D1642336

ROTHERHAM PUBLIC LIBRARIES

GREAT BATTLES AND SIEGES

WATERLOO

PHILIP SAUVAIN

ILLUSTRATIONS BY
TONY GIBBONS & FRED ANDERSON

A ZOË BOOK

GREAT BATTLES

A ZOË BOOK

©1993 Zoë Books Limited

Devised and produced by
Zoë Books Limited
15 Worthy Lane
Winchester
Hampshire SO23 7AB
England

First published in Great Britain in 1993 by
Zoë Books Limited
15 Worthy Lane
Winchester
Hampshire SO23 7AB

A CIP catalogue record for this book is available from the British Library.

ISBN 1 874488 08 8

Printed in Italy
Design: Julian Holland Publishing Ltd
Picture research: Victoria Sturgess
Illustrations: Tony Gibbons and Fred Anderson
Production: Grahame Griffiths

Photographic acknowledgements
The publishers wish to acknowledge, with thanks, the following photographic sources:
The Bridgeman Art Library/Christie's 7b; The Bridgeman Art
Library/Victoria and Albert Museum 20; The Bridgeman Art Library/United
Services Club 24;
Hulton-Deutsch Collection Ltd 4, 6, 7t, 12, 13t, 17, 25;
Leeds City Art Galleries 21;
Courtesy of the Director, National Army Museum London 15, 18, 19, 26, 27t;
Peter Newark's Military Pictures 5, 13b, 27b, 28b, 29;
Courtesy of the Trustees of the Royal Green Jackets Museum 16;
Philip Sauvain 28t;
Courtesy of the Board of Trustees of the Victoria and Albert Museum Cover, 9, 11, 22.

WATERLOO

Contents

The ambition of one man

Waterloo, Belgium. Sunday night, 18 June 1815. A British army officer remembered waking up at about midnight. 'I got up to look around a battlefield by the pale moonlight. All day long it had been the place of noise and strife. Now it was so calm and still. Long I continued to gaze on this sad and solemn scene. All this slaughter to gratify the ambition of one man.' The 'one man' was the French Emperor Napoleon, one of the greatest leaders in history. He was then only 45 years of age, yet his career was over. That day, he had been defeated at the Battle of Waterloo.

Napoleon Bonaparte was born in Corsica, a French island in the Mediterranean Sea, in 1769. He entered the army and was so successful that he became a **general** when he was only 24 years old. In 1796-97 Napoleon led the French army in Italy and won several great victories against the Austrians. Napoleon saw himself as a future leader of France.

▶ *Napoleon Bonaparte made a surprise invasion of northern Italy in 1800, after crossing the Alps.*

WATERLOO

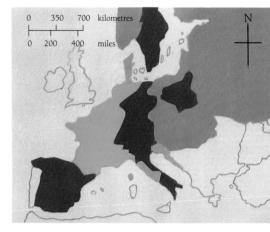

◀ Napoleon had a special affection for the Imperial Guard, who had fought with him in so many of his battles. After his abdication, he said farewell to them at **Fontainebleau** on 20 April 1814.

In November 1799 he used his power as a general to take over the government. He became the leader, or **First Consul,** of the French **republic.** Five years later Napoleon was crowned Emperor of France.

The French people worshipped Napoleon. He defeated the Austrians and the Russians at the Battle of Austerlitz and the **Prussians** at the Battle of Jena. By 1811 most of Europe was under French control. Only Britain was undefeated, largely because of the strength of its Royal Navy. Britain had defeated France in 1805 at the great sea battle of Trafalgar.

Until 1808, Britain had done little fighting on land, although it had given large sums of money to help the armies of Europe to fight France. When Napoleon invaded Spain and Portugal, however, the British sent a small army against him. It was led by Sir Arthur Wellesley, the future Duke of Wellington. The British forces defeated the French in the **Peninsular War.** Wellington then invaded France itself, in 1814.

By this time, Napoleon had been defeated in other parts of Europe too. He made his biggest mistake when he invaded Russia in 1812. The severe Russian winter trapped his army. Many soldiers died of cold and starvation, and very few returned home. Napoleon could not recover from the disaster. In 1813, his new army of nearly 200 000 men was beaten by 300 000 Russians, Prussians, Austrians and Swedes at the Battle of Leipzig, and one year later his enemies were riding into Paris.

Napoleon was forced to give up his claim to the French throne, to **abdicate.** In his farewell speech to his finest and most loyal soldiers, the **Imperial Guard** (also called the **Old Guard**) on 20 April 1814, he said, 'Soldiers, I bid you farewell. We have been together for twenty years. Your conduct has always been all that I could wish for. Be loyal to your new king and to your new officers as well. Do not forsake the country you love. Adieu, my children. In my heart I shall always be with you. Do not forget me!'

French Empire

Areas dependent on France and ruled by Napoleon's relatives and supporters

Napoleon's allies

▲ Napoleon controlled most of Europe in 1811. Some countries, such as Belgium, were made part of the French Empire. Some, such as Spain, were ruled by one of Napoleon's family. Others, such as Russia, were forced to sign a treaty of friendship with France.

Emperor in exile

Napoleon was allowed to retire in peace to the small island of **Elba,** off the coast of Italy. He became the island's ruler, and kept his title of Emperor. He was also allowed to take about 400 soldiers of the Old Guard to Elba with him, and these soldiers were joined by another 500 or 600 volunteers.

Napoleon was still a young man. It was too much to expect a man of his energy and great talents to stay on a tiny island for the rest of his life. He decided to escape. On 26 February 1815, Napoleon left Elba in secret with his small army of only 1000 men. They landed near Antibes on the French coast on 1 March. Napoleon then started the long march towards Paris. He went first to Grenoble and to Lyons. Newspaper headlines told the people of Paris about his progress. 'The Tiger has broken out of his lair.' 'The Monster has been three days at sea.' 'The Wretch has landed.' **Marshal** Ney, one of Napoleon's most trusted commanders, told the new French king, Louis XVIII, that he would bring Napoleon back to Paris 'in an iron cage.'

▼ *On 26 February, 1815, Napoleon escaped from Elba with a handful of his supporters. Three days later they landed in secret on the coast of the French Riviera.*

WATERLOO

However, Ney, like many other French soldiers, was soon charmed by Napoleon and changed sides. Ney and his men joined Napoleon's growing army as it neared Paris. The newspaper headlines began to change. The man who had been 'The Buzzard' in Antibes became 'The Invader' in Grenoble. By the time Napoleon reached Lyons he was simply 'The General'. On his arrival in Paris itself, he became 'His Imperial Majesty' and 'The Emperor'.

Napoleon had become a hero once more. On 20 March 1815, he rode through the streets of Paris in an open carriage, to the cheers of thousands of people. It had taken him only twenty days to recapture France. Not a shot had been fired. Not a blow had been struck. The new king, Louis XVIII, fled. The National Guard, which a day earlier had cried *'Vive le Roi'* ('Long live the King') for Louis XVIII, now shouted *'Vive l'Empereur'* ('Long live the Emperor') for Napoleon.

While Napoleon was in exile on Elba, the rulers of Europe held a conference. It was called the **Congress of Vienna.** The rulers met to decide what to do with Napoleon's empire. Now they had to decide what to do about Napoleon himself. They agreed to send their armed forces into battle against him again. Two of these armies began to assemble in Belgium, close to the French border. One army was led by the British **Field Marshal**, the Duke of Wellington. The other was led by the Prussian Field Marshal, Prince von Blücher.

▲ *Napoleon returned to Paris on 20 March 1815, three weeks after leaving Elba.*

◀ *Scenes like this, where Napoleon was welcomed with open arms by former soldiers, were a common sight as he made his way in triumph towards Paris.*

The Army of the North

Napoleon knew that his enemies would attack France as soon as they were ready. He and his officers worked feverishly to raise a large army in the shortest possible time. France had been at war for over 20 years. Many of the men Napoleon called on to join the army had already trained as soldiers and fought for France. It took him only twelve weeks to recruit the soldiers he needed, and to divide them into separate armies to defend France's frontiers.

Napoleon's task was to stop the enemy armies from invading France from four or five different directions at once. He decided to deal with the British and the Prussian armies in the Low Countries first, since they were the nearest. If Britain and Prussia could be forced to agree to a peace, Austria and Russia might do so as well. If not, he would fight each army in turn. This is why he chose 125 000 of his finest soldiers to form the Army of the North. They assembled in secret, close to the Belgian border. Napoleon himself left Paris at 3.00 am on Monday 12 June, to take command.

▲ This map shows how the armies of Napoleon, Ney, Grouchy, Blücher and Wellington took different routes in Belgium before the Battle of Waterloo.

▲ The French army wore distinctive uniforms in 1815. Armies in those days wore bright, eye-catching colours which made them stand out on the battlefield, instead of helping to conceal them.

WATERLOO

◀ *Field Marshal Prince von Blücher, commander of the Prussian army*

Facing Napoleon were 113 000 Prussians, led by Blücher, and a mixed British, Belgian, Dutch and German army of about 70 000 to 80 000 soldiers, led by Wellington. The French were outnumbered by nearly two to one. However, Napoleon was confident that his soldiers could win. They were all French, so commands would be quickly understood because they all spoke the same language. They were highly trained, so they knew exactly what to do. Above all, they were fighting for their country against an enemy which was about to invade France. Napoleon was sure that he could count on his soldiers' loyalty.

The soldiers of the French army *were* devoted to Napoleon. He had won many great victories in the past, and they expected him to do the same now. Napoleon looked after his men. He made sure of their welfare and comfort, talked to the wounded and he made a point of remembering their names. Men were promoted because they had earned it, not because they were rich or came from a noble family.

By contrast, only one third of the soldiers in Wellington's army were British. Another third came from Germany and the rest spoke Dutch, French or Flemish. Most of the men in the British regiments were experienced **regular soldiers** who joined up because they were paid to fight. However, only a few of them had fought with Wellington in the Peninsular War. Some of the German soldiers were also first class troops but others were unreliable. (During the battle some even fired at their own officers). Wellington also had doubts about the loyalty of his French-speaking Belgian soldiers. Belgium had been part of Napoleon's empire for 20 years, and many of these troops preferred Napoleon to Wellington as a leader.

'The scum of the earth'

Unlike Napoleon, Wellington did not have a high opinion of the worth of his own soldiers. He once called them 'the scum of the earth' and said 'they have all enlisted for drink.' On another occasion he said, 'I don't know what they'll do to the enemy, but my goodness they scare me!' Even so, when these soldiers helped him to win his victories, he called them 'worthy fellows' and after Waterloo he said, 'I never saw the British **infantry** (foot soldiers) behave so well.'

Wellington's soldiers obeyed orders, not because they were devoted to him as leader, but because they knew the penalty for disobeying. At that time, discipline in the British army was harsh and cruel. Men were flogged with a vicious whip, the cat o'nine tails, or hanged if they broke the rules. The pay was low, the food was poor and the living conditions were appalling. Diseases soon spread among the troops, yet living conditions in the slums of big cities such as London were often worse than this. There was no shortage of **recruits** for the army.

▼ *The Duchess of Richmond's Ball, Thursday, 15 June 1815, is probably the most famous ball in history. It was here that the Duke of Wellington and his leading officers first learned of the seriousness of the Allied position.*

WATERLOO

The Duke of Wellington was born in Ireland in 1769. He was the same age as his enemy, Napoleon. Wellington entered the British army as an officer. He served as an army commander in India and then in the Peninsular War, where he won a series of great victories in Portugal and Spain between 1808 and 1814. Wellington was a cautious leader who took no unnecessary risks. This is why he was respected by his men, even if they did not like him. They called him 'Nosey' and they feared the discipline he imposed. They did not give him the affection and the loyalty which the French soldiers gave to Napoleon.

Most of Wellington's officers came from the rich or noble upper classes. They bought their position, or **commission,** in the army. Many of the top jobs in the army went to people who had paid for them. Their rank often depended more on their wealth and the people they knew in high places than on their ability to lead soldiers well in battle.

In 1815, Wellington knew that Napoleon was about to invade Belgium but he did not know when or where. In order to stop people panicking, he and many of his leading officers attended a ball given by the Duchess of Richmond in Brussels on Thursday night, 15 June. During the evening, news came that Napoleon's army had seized Charleroi, a town only 50 kilometres (30 miles) away. Wellington retired to a private room with some of his officers. Pointing to a map, he said, 'Napoleon has humbugged me! He has gained twenty-four hours march ...'.

On the following day, 16 June, a section of the French army, led by Marshal Ney, attacked an important cross-roads called **Quatre Bras** ('Four Arms'). *Quatre Bras* lay between Wellington's army and the Prussian army led by Field Marshal Blücher. Ney aimed at cutting the road link between the two army commanders.

▲ *Soldiers of the British (left) and Prussian (right) armies.*

▲ *Field Marshal the Duke of Wellington. Like Napoleon, Wellington showed his talents as a military leader at a very early age. He was promoted to the high rank of Major-General when he was only 33 years old.*

Quatre Bras

Napoleon had decided to strike hard at Wellington's and Blücher's weakest point – the gap between the two Allied armies. On 16 June he led his soldiers in a massive attack against the Prussians at Ligny, while Ney attacked Wellington at *Quatre Bras*. In this way, Napoleon hoped to keep the two Allied armies apart.

He knew that his soldiers would be greatly outnumbered if he allowed Wellington and Blücher to attack the French army together on the same battlefield at the same time. It was essential to keep them apart at all costs. If he could do this, he was confident he could beat either army on its own.

In fact, things did not go according to plan. Wellington held *Quatre Bras* all day. Ney was too cautious – he failed to see the weakness of Wellington's position. He thought there were more Allied troops than there really were. Meanwhile, Wellington decided to fall back towards a long low hill, or ridge, called *Mont St Jean*, which overlooked a wide valley close to the village of Waterloo.

▼ *The Belgian village of* Quatre Bras *in 1815*

WATERLOO

To cover the fact that his army was retreating, Wellington bluffed Ney into thinking that the whole of the Allied army was at *Quatre Bras*. Ney took too long to realize that only a thin line of **cavalry** and a small number of horse-drawn guns still faced the French lines. When the French did advance in strength, the British guns opened fire and then galloped away, taking advantage of a sudden storm. An officer in charge of one of the guns said there was, '... an awful clap of thunder, and lightning that almost blinded us. The rain came down as if a water- spout had broken over us. We galloped for our lives through the storm. Away we went, helter-skelter, guns and cavalrymen all mixed, going like mad and covering each other with mud to be washed off by the rain.'

The French failed to prevent the retreat of Wellington's army. When Napoleon reached Waterloo later that day and saw that Wellington's men were in a strong position, he was very angry. 'You have ruined France!' he told Ney.

Napoleon himself had had much greater success than Ney. He had cut the Prussian army in two at the Battle of Ligny, which forced Blücher to retreat towards the north. Napoleon now thought that he had driven the wedge he needed between the two Allied armies. To make sure, he ordered Marshal Grouchy, commanding 33 000 men on the right side of the French army, to prevent Blücher from linking up with Wellington.

Grouchy was not the best man for the job. He had no imagination and was too slow to issue effective orders. He had no idea where the Prussians were! He failed to stop Blücher from carrying out a promise made earlier to Wellington – that he would send Prussian troops to join Wellington the next day. As a result, Blücher was able to swing his troops round and move a large part of the Prussian army westwards towards Wellington at Waterloo. This was the very thing that Napoleon had tried so hard to block.

▲ *Marshal Ney was a brave but rash commander. He led the left wing of the French army at* Quatre Bras *and later commanded the main assault on the Allied army at Waterloo. He was later shot as a traitor because he had withdrawn his support from Louis XVIII and given it to Napoleon.*

▼ *The Battle of* Quatre Bras

The battlefield at Waterloo

THE TWO ARMIES AT WATERLOO

WELLINGTON'S SOLDIERS

50 000 infantry *
12 500 cavalry **
5 500 gunners
68 000 Total

156 guns

Of these 68 000 soldiers: 24 000 were British, 26 000 were German, 18 000 were Dutch or Belgian

NAPOLEON'S SOLDIERS

49 000 infantry
16 000 cavalry
7 000 gunners
72 000 Total

246 guns

Almost all of Napoleon's 72 000 soldiers were French

(* infantry fight on foot:
** cavalry fight on horseback)

The position which Wellington had chosen to defend was above a valley about three to five kilometres (two to three miles) long and about 800 metres (half a mile) wide. The sides of the valley consisted of low ridges. Wellington's army camped on the ridge of *Mont St Jean* to the north, while Napoleon's army camped on the ridge to the south. The guns, or **artillery,** of both sides later bombarded each other all day long from the tops of these low hills. Infantry and cavalry charges had to be made across the valley floor and then up the slope on the other side.

The main road running north and south between Brussels and Charleroi ran almost exactly through the middle of the battle area. It divided both Wellington's and Napoleon's armies in two. Napoleon intended to use this road to march on Brussels, the Belgian capital.

Wellington had the better position on the battlefield. His plan for the day was simple. He would hold the ridge until the arrival of the Prussian soldiers gave him the advantage in men and guns which he needed.

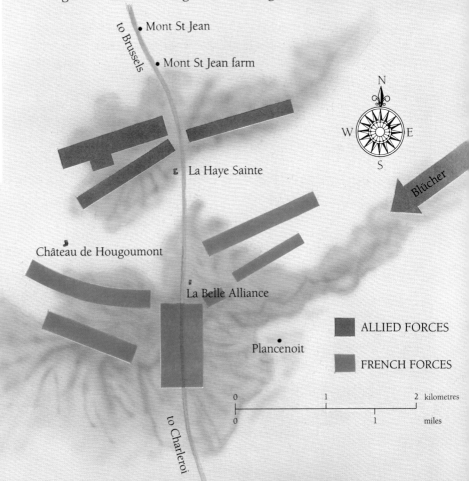

▶ *The Battle of Waterloo*

WATERLOO

He expected them at midday, but it was mid-afternoon before they were able to take part in the fighting. The troops on the right hand side of Wellington's army, his right flank, were defending the village of *Merbe Braine* and a steep-sided valley. The village and the valley provided good cover for these soldiers. Wellington had earlier stationed 17 000 soldiers in two villages further to the west. This was because he expected Napoleon to swing his army round to attack his right flank from that direction. To the east, on Wellington's left flank, were two small villages, *La Haye* and *Papelotte*. The buildings in these villages also gave cover to the soldiers defending them.

◀ *The village of Waterloo in 1815*

In front of Wellington, on the south-facing slope of the valley, were a number of fortified farms. Wellington stationed troops in these buildings to hold up the French advance. The most important buildings were the **Château de Hougoumont** to his right, and a large farmhouse, **La Haye Sainte,** to his left. *La Haye Sainte* was the smaller of the two buildings. When it was captured by the French at 6.00 pm, it soon proved troublesome to Wellington's left side.

The *Château de Hougoumont* had a number of out-buildings, a garden and a small wood. Wellington stationed soldiers from the Guards there, together with some of the German soldiers. If they could hold on there, the French would find it hard to mount an attack on his right flank.

◀ **La Belle Alliance** *was the farmhouse which Napoleon used as his headquarters during the battle.*

Sunday morning, 18 June 1815

On the night before the battle, Wellington's soldiers tried to get some rest. However, pouring rain made sleep almost impossible. A soldier later described what happened. '... We could not use our blankets, the ground was too wet to lie down,' he wrote. 'We sat on our knapsacks until daylight without fires. There was no shelter from the weather. The water ran in streams from the cuffs of our jackets. In short, we were as wet as if we had been plunged over head in a river. We had one consolation. We knew the enemy were in the same plight.'

When dawn broke on Sunday, 18 June 1815, few of the soldiers on either side were comfortable. Both armies had had very little sleep during the wet and stormy night. They were soaked to the skin. 'We were drenched with rain, benumbed and shaking with the cold,' wrote an officer. [The ground] 'was nearly ankle-deep in water. Comfort was out of the question.'

The rain eased off by about 9.00 am and the skies became clearer. Both sides now had time to inspect each other's positions. Wellington had grouped his soldiers in two lines on the low hill overlooking the wide valley. The main line of soldiers was on top of the ridge. The other was kept in reserve and stationed just below the slope on the other side

▼ *Wellington rode through the Allied lines on the morning of the battle. As you can see from the bedraggled soldiers and the waterlogged ground, it had only just stopped raining.*

WATERLOO

▲ *Thick mud made it impossible to move the heavy cannon into position.*

of the hill. This meant that, if they kept their heads down, most of the French cannonballs went over them. Napoleon could not see these troops since they were below the slope. He would get no warning, therefore, if and when Wellington re-grouped the troops for an attack.

Napoleon's forces were also drawn up in two main lines, but he kept his best soldiers, the Imperial Guard, in the rear as a reserve. These could be brought up rapidly to strengthen any part of the front which was weakening or where an extra thrust was needed.

Wellington inspected his lines before the battle started. He made sure there were adequate supplies of ammunition and that the arrangements for looking after the wounded were satisfactory. During the battle Wellington rode a small chestnut horse called Copenhagen. He spent some time on the highest ground above the battlefield with his staff, so that he could see what was going on, but also rode into the thick of the fighting to encourage his men.

Napoleon stationed himself during the battle on a small hill near a farmhouse called *La Belle Alliance.* Here he had a large table spread with maps and plans. He used his telescope to keep an eye on his troops and on the enemy.

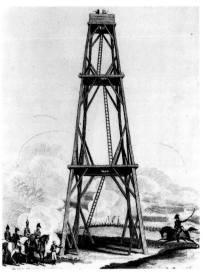

▲ *Napoleon watched the progress of the battle through a telescope. His staff had rigged up this wooden tower to give him a better view.*

The Château de Hougoumont

The waterlogged ground had an important effect on the battle at Waterloo. It delayed the arrival of the Prussian troops which Blücher had promised would arrive at midday, and it delayed the start of the battle itself. Napoleon was told that his heavy guns would soon be bogged down in mud if he began the attack before the ground dried out. The cannonballs would also sink into the mud, instead of bouncing along the ground and doing much more damage. So Napoleon did not make his first attack until nearly noon. Had he started at 9.00 am, however, he could have defeated Wellington long before the Prussians arrived.

At 11.35 am French troops began to attack the *Château de Hougoumont*. Napoleon knew that Wellington would be expecting an attack on his right wing. He wanted Wellington to think that this was the direction from which the main French attack would come. **Column** after column of French soldiers came down the north-facing ridge and attempted to storm the *Château*. But the attack failed, despite the courage of the French soldiers.

▼ *The* Château de Hougoumont *during the fighting at Waterloo.*

WATERLOO

◀ *The strong Allied defence of the* Château de Hougoumont *made it difficult for Napoleon to mount an attack on the Allied right wing.*

Soldiers from the British Guards regiments and from the German states of **Hanover** and **Nassau** defended *Hougoumont* well. They held on to it all day, despite heavy casualties. In fact, Wellington needed only 3500 soldiers to defend *Hougoumont,* while Napoleon wasted 14000 men in a fruitless effort to take the building. *Hougoumont* remained a problem for Napoleon throughout the battle. The walls of the *Château* gave cover to the British guns, enabling them to fire at French troops across the valley.

Nonetheless, the French attack on *Hougoumont* was still only a trick. Napoleon hoped that it would draw some of Wellington's troops away from the centre of the battlefield. This was where he intended to direct his main attack. He aimed to split Wellington's army in two – just as he had done to Blücher's Prussians only two days earlier.

Four columns of infantry – about 18000 men– together with cavalry and 74 guns were assembled to launch an attack on the centre of Wellington's line. They were led by Marshal Ney. The aim was to capture *La Haye Sainte* in the valley and the farm of *Mont St Jean* on the ridge. The Allied left wing would then be cut off from the rest of Wellington's army. It would be out of touch with its commander and unable to retreat to Brussels. If it fell back towards the east, the Allied soldiers would soon cause confusion and panic in the Prussian ranks. This would make it even more difficult for Blücher to come to Wellington's aid. Once the Allied army was split in two, Napoleon believed that Wellington would have to retreat. French soldiers could then pursue them, cut them to pieces and force the British out of the war.

The attack on Mont St Jean

The attack on the village of *Mont St Jean* began at about 1.00 pm. Ney positioned the 74 guns on a low ridge in the middle of the valley. It was about 700 metres from the British front line. Columns of French foot soldiers passed between the guns. As they marched down the slope, the guns above them opened fire and bombarded the British positions in the middle. A British soldier described what happened. 'The air was suffocatingly hot. We were wrapped in dense smoke. So thick was the hail of balls and bullets, it seemed dangerous to put out an arm lest it be torn off.'

When the gunfire ceased, the French infantry attacked. The advance broke a brigade of Dutch and Belgian troops who turned and fled. As the French reached the top of the ridge, however, they came face to face with two Allied brigades commanded by General Picton. He ordered his men to fire and then to charge the French with their bayonets. Picton was shot dead but the British charge threw the French into confusion.

▼ *Napoleon's view of the Battle of Waterloo. Notice the French cannon. Napoleon had five guns for every three of Wellington's.*

WATERLOO

It was at this moment that the Scots **Greys** and other British cavalry units came down the hill like a whirlwind and drove the French infantry back. They cut them down with their sabres. They drove the French so far back that they also cut down the French gunners 700 metres away. Those guns remained out of action for the rest of the day. Napoleon ordered an immediate **counter-attack**, and the British cavalry suffered heavy casualties as they were driven back. Despite these heavy losses, the French had so far been unable to make any real headway. They were no nearer to fulfilling Napoleon's main aim – to split Wellington's forces in two. The Allies still commanded the slopes of *Mont St Jean,* and *Hougoumont* and *La Haye Sainte* still held out against the French.

The next stage of the battle began when Napoleon's gunners opened fire again on the British lines. Yet despite the massive **gun barrage**, the soldiers stood firm. Already they could see help at hand. The first of the Prussian soldiers could be seen on the skyline to the east. After this heavy **bombardment**, however, Marshal Ney made a terrible mistake. Through the gunfire smoke in the distance, he could just make out with his telescope that enemy wagons and soldiers seemed to be pulling back towards Brussels. In fact the wagons were carrying the wounded and the troops were taking up fresh positions to shelter from the French guns. Ney was not to know this. He decided that Wellington had ordered a retreat. Without thinking, and without consulting Napoleon, he told his best horsemen, the *cuirassiers* to charge the British guns. It was now about 4.00 pm. Four thousand cavalry moved forwards and mounted the ridge. As they did so, they came face to face with the British **squares.**

▲ *The charge of the Scots Greys. They put the French infantry to flight but suffered heavy losses when the French lancers launched a counter-attack.*

The British squares

A British officer who fought at Waterloo admired the French cavalry as they came forward. He said, 'Their first charge was magnificent. As soon as they quickened their trot into a gallop, the cuirassiers bent their heads, so that ... they seemed cased in armour from the plume to the saddle.'

Facing a cavalry charge like this was very frightening for a foot soldier. However, Wellington had worked out a way of dealing with such a charge. He formed his foot soldiers, the infantry, into squares. On each of the four sides, soldiers at the front knelt down to fire their rifles. A line of soldiers behind them fired over their shoulders, while behind them stood a third line of soldiers, ready to take the place of anyone in front who fell. The horse-drawn guns were placed between these squares.

The French cavalry **squadrons** had to charge forward through a hail of bullets and cannon shot. A gunner at Waterloo described what happened. 'I saw through the smoke the leading squadrons coming on at a brisk trot. On our part every man stood steadily at his post, the guns ready. I allowed them to advance unchallenged until the head of the column might have been about fifty or sixty yards (50 metres) from us. Then I gave the word, "Fire!" The effect was terrible. Nearly the whole leading rank fell at once. The ground blocked with victims of the first attack now became almost impassable.'

▼ *The French cavalry charging uphill towards the British squares were driven back time and time again.*

WATERLOO

▲ *A British 9-pounder gun of the type used at Waterloo.*

Marshal Ney's cavalry attacked again and again like this, each time with heavy loss of life. Ney himself led many of the charges. Four times his horse was killed under him as he rode towards the British lines.

Each time the British squares held firm. An officer who fought in the battle said the loss of life among the French cavalry was so great, that the British infantry began to mock them. 'Here come these fools again!', they shouted. Napoleon, watching the action through his telescope, began to despair. 'Will the English never show their backs?' he complained. He ordered a second major attack at about 5.00 pm with fresh cavalry. More than 9000 horsemen charged the British lines in repeated attacks. All were beaten back.

The British resistance was bought at a terrible price. The ground inside the squares was littered with the bodies of hundreds of dead or wounded soldiers. Cannonballs had torn holes in the squares, only to be filled immediately by a soldier behind. A soldier later wrote, 'It was now to be seen which side would stand killing longest. The Duke visited us frequently during this period. He was always cool. "Hard pounding this, gentlemen," he said to one unit. "We will see who can pound longest."'

Blücher to the rescue

By late afternoon, large numbers of Prussian soldiers had begun to attack the French lines from the east. They directed their attack on the village of **Plancenoit.** If they took it, they might soon be able to cut off the French line of retreat. Napoleon had to weaken his attack on the British lines by taking soldiers away to deal with the Prussian threat. Above all, he now needed a quick victory over Wellington. This is why he ordered an all-out attack on *La Haye Sainte.* The farm fell at last at 6.00 pm, mainly because the soldiers defending it had run out of ammunition. The French immediately moved guns into the farmhouse. They bombarded the British lines so heavily that they broke up some of the British squares.

▲ *The presence of Napoleon on the battlefield inspired soldiers to great deeds. The Imperial Guard saluted him as they marched past to make the last all-out attack on the Allied lines.*

Napoleon then decided that the time had come to use his finest troops, the Imperial Guard. They would launch an all-out attack on Wellington. It was already early evening, and would soon be dark. There was no time to lose. At about 7.00 pm, Napoleon mounted his white **charger** and formed his **veteran** soldiers into two columns. As they rode or filed past him, he pointed his arm towards Wellington. The soldiers answered him with the cry, *'Vive l'Empereur!'*

WATERLOO

Marshal Ney himself, with sword in hand, led the soldiers of the Old Guard up the crest of the hill. In the confusion no one could later remember exactly what happened. One popular story was that the Guardsmen defending that part of the British lines had been lying down to escape the French gunfire. When the French cavalry reached the top of the slope, all they could see was the Duke of Wellington with a number of his staff officers in the distance. They spurred on their horses, thinking they had won, until Wellington shouted the order 'Up, Guards, and at 'em!' Instantly, the Guards rose to their feet. This surprised the leading French cavalry so much that they paused. It gave the British soldiers the chance to fire volley after volley into the French ranks.

Both sides were now exhausted. Wellington correctly sensed that the French were beaten. The time had come for him to sound the general advance. He waved his cocked hat in the air and pointed it towards the French. The Allied soldiers, who had been under attack all day, responded strongly. They pushed forward, together with the Prussian army from the east. They broke up the French ranks and routed Napoleon's once splendid army. Napoleon prepared to die on the battlefield but Marshal Soult seized the bridle of his horse and urged him to withdraw. 'Sire, are not the enemy already lucky enough?' he said. The retreat to Paris had begun.

After over-running the French positions, Wellington and most of his army turned back towards Waterloo. They left the pursuit of the French to Blücher. The Prussians were fresh, and ready to take revenge on the men who had defeated them at Ligny only two days earlier.

▼ *After pursuing the French, Wellington rode back along the road to Waterloo. At about 10.00 pm that evening he met up with Field Marshal Blücher. The picture shows them meeting at Napoleon's headquarters,* La Belle Alliance, *but Wellington himself denied that this meeting took place.*

Victory!

Wellington returned to his headquarters in the village of Waterloo. Now that the battle was over he was able to see the extent of the casualties and the misery of the wounded men lying on the battlefield. There were 15 000 British dead and wounded, 7000 Prussian and 29 000 French. The fact that nearly one third of the Allied casualties were Prussian showed how important Blücher's army had been in securing victory.

▲ *About 50 000 dead or injured soldiers lay on the battlefield at the end of the Battle of Waterloo. It took four days to take away all the wounded. The peace which followed in Europe had been bought at a terrible price.*

Afterwards, Wellington enquired about his friends. He was distressed to be told that many had been killed or seriously wounded. He wrote in a letter, 'My heart is broken by the terrible loss I have sustained in my old friends and companions, and my poor soldiers. Believe me, nothing except a battle lost, can be half so sad as a battle won.'

News of the victory at Waterloo reached Britain a few days later. An artist called Benjamin Haydon was in Portman Street in the centre of London when the news arrived. An official messenger told him, 'The Duke has beat Napoleon, taken one hundred and fifty pieces of cannon, and is marching to Paris.' The news spread rapidly. A great crowd assembled in St James's Square. Haydon said they sang 'God save the King' and 'filled the place with shouts and huzzas.' In a village in the English Lake District, Dorothy Wordsworth, sister of the poet William Wordsworth, thought the celebrations were wrong since so many soldiers had been killed. She wrote, 'The details of the battle of the 18th are dreadful. I have no patience with the tinkling of our Ambleside bells.'

Nearly three weeks after the battle, on 7 July 1815, the Allied troops rode into Paris once again. It was exactly one hundred days since

WATERLOO

◀ *Wellington broke down when he read the casualty lists after the battle. Tears ran down his cheeks as he listened to the surgeon's report. He knew many of the men on the list personally. Some were among his best friends.*

Napoleon had landed in France earlier in the year. Now he had failed for the last time. He had underestimated the ability of the British squares to stand up to the onslaught of the French cavalry. He had also been misled into thinking that Blücher and the Prussians would not be able to come to Wellington's aid. Thousands of the finest soldiers in France had been slaughtered charging the Allied lines. It had all been in vain.

Wellington said his victory had been 'The nearest run thing that you ever saw.' Had the British squares hesitated, the history of Europe might have taken a different turn. As it was, after 23 years of almost continuous fighting, Europe was at last at peace. The Allied victory at Waterloo had brought to an end the period of the Napoleonic Wars. In fact, there was no general warfare in Europe on the scale of the Napoleonic Wars until the outbreak of the First World War in 1914.

▼ *The Allies entered Paris on 7 July 1815. Wellington had to stop Blücher from destroying a bridge across the Seine, which had been named after Napoleon's victory over the Prussians at the Battle of Jena.*

Exile to St Helena

Napoleon narrowly escaped capture by Blücher's Prussians who would have shot him on sight. He gave up the throne of France for the second time, and at Rochefort on the west coast of France, he took refuge in a British warship, the *Bellerophon*. When the ship moored in Falmouth harbour in Cornwall, hundreds of people went out in small boats to see it.

Some of Napoleon's friends said that he wanted to live in Britain as a country squire, but this was not to be! Nor was he allowed to fulfil a dream of going to the United States of America. Instead, he was treated as a prisoner of war and was transferred to another ship, the *Northumberland*. After some discussion, the Allies agreed that he should be exiled to the small, rocky island of **St Helena** in the middle of the South Atlantic Ocean. This island is nearly 2000 kilometres (over 1200 miles) from the nearest mainland of West Africa.

Napoleon arrived at St Helena on 15 October 1815, less than eight months after leaving Elba in February. Escape from St Helena was out of the question. His stay there was comfortable but not luxurious, and he had many complaints. He made friends with some of the British residents on St Helena, and he began to write his *Memoirs*. In them he boasted about his achievements. 'Had I succeeded, I would have died with the reputation of the greatest man that ever existed. As it is, although I have failed, I shall be considered as an extraordinary man. I have fought fifty pitched battles, almost all of which I have won. I raised myself from nothing to be the most powerful monarch in the world. Europe was at my feet.' Wellington himself said of Napoleon that, 'his presence on the field made the difference of forty thousand men.'

▲ *Wellington's great victory was commemorated in many different ways. Hundreds of towns, streets, buildings and roads were named Wellington (such as the capital of New Zealand) or Waterloo (such as one of London's leading railway stations). Many statues of Wellington were erected, including this one close to his London home of Apsley House (now the Wellington Museum).*

▶ *Napoleon on board HMS* Bellerophon. *Wisely, Napoleon had taken refuge on a British ship. Blücher wanted to shoot him on sight.*

WATERLOO

◀ *One glance at St Helena told Napoleon there would be no escape this time.*

After living for six years on St Helena, Napoleon died there in 1821. He was 51 years old. Twenty years later, in 1840, the British Government allowed the French to take his remains back to France for burial in the *Hôtel des Invalides* in Paris. By this time, Napoleon was again regarded by the French people as the country's greatest hero.

By contrast, Napoleon's chief opponent at Waterloo, the Duke of Wellington, lost much of his popularity when he became Prime Minister in 1828. Mobs even stoned his house. At that time, many people wanted to reform the way in which Members of Parliament were elected. Wellington, however, did not believe in giving ordinary people the vote.

As Wellington grew older, people began to respect him again for his triumph as the hero of Waterloo. When he died in 1852, at the age of 83, Wellington was given a magnificent state funeral and was buried in London's St Paul's Cathedral.

▼ *Napoleon dictated his* Memoirs *soon after arriving on St Helena.*

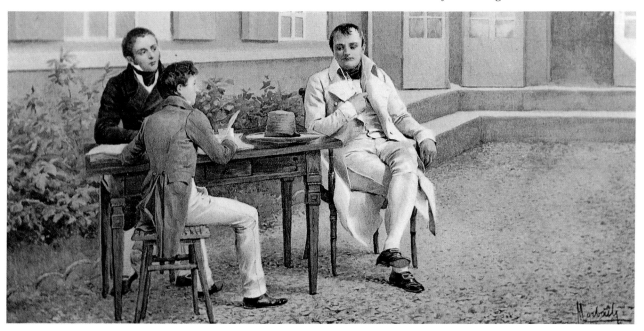

Glossary

abdicate: to give up a throne

artillery: guns

bombardment: constant gunfire directed at a single target

cavalry: soldiers who fight on horseback

charger: a large horse, chosen for its strength, and used by cavalrymen to ride into battle

Château de Hougoumont: a large fortified house on the western side of the battlefield at Waterloo which was defended by British soldiers

column: soldiers who advance in a long line, one after the other, instead of on a wide front

commission: an official document, appointing an officer to one of the armed services

Congress of Vienna: a meeting of the leaders of Europe which decided what to do with the lands which had been conquered by Napoleon. It met in the Austrian capital, Vienna, between 1814 and 1815

counter-attack: an attack launched by an army after it has itself been attacked

cuirassiers: mounted soldiers who wore a cuirass – a piece of armour made of steel or leather which covered the chest and the back

Elba: a small island off the coast of Italy

Field Marshal: the highest ranking officer in the British army

First Consul: the title which Napoleon took when he seized power as leader of the French republic in 1799

Fontainebleau: town with a royal palace, about 55 kilometres (35 miles) south-east of Paris

General: a high ranking officer outranked only by a Marshal or Field Marshal

Greys: British cavalry soldiers, so named because they rode grey horses

gun barrage: see **bombardment**

Hanover: a state in northern Germany, ruled by the British monarchy until 1837

Imperial Guard: the finest and most experienced soldiers in France. Some had fought with Napoleon since his earliest campaigns

infantry: soldiers who fight on foot

La Belle Alliance: the farmhouse used by Napoleon as his headquarters during the Battle of Waterloo

La Haye Sainte: a farmhouse on the eastern side of the centre of the battlefield at Waterloo. It was defended by British soldiers but was captured by the French

Marshal: the highest ranking officer in the French army

Nassau: a state in central Germany

Old Guard: soldiers of the Imperial Guard

Peninsular War: the war against France which was fought in the Iberian Peninsula (Spain and Portugal) between 1808 and 1814

Plancenoit: a French-held village to the east of the battlefield at Waterloo which was attacked by the Prussians

Prussians: people from Prussia – an independent state in what is now north-eastern Germany (and also partly in Poland)

Quatre Bras: a village at the important cross-roads south of Waterloo on the main Brussels to Charleroi road

recruits: soldiers who are new to the army and are not yet fully trained

WATERLOO

regular soldier: a professional soldier who enlists in the army for a long time

republic: a country which is not ruled by a monarch

squadron: at Waterloo this was used to describe a group of mounted soldiers

square: at Waterloo this meant foot soldiers who stood two or three deep in a square, so that they could direct their fire against attack from any direction

St Helena: a small, rocky island in the middle of the South Atlantic Ocean

veteran: an old soldier

Further Reading

A Soldier in Wellington's Army, by Fiona Somerset Fry, Wayland, 1987

Napoleon, by A. Blackwood, Wayland, 1986

Napoleon, by Nathaniel Harris, Batsford Educational, 1986

Spotlight on The Napoleonic Wars, by Nathaniel Harris, Wayland, 1987

The French Revolution and Napoleon, by Stephen Pratt, Wayland, 1992

'The French Revolution and the Napoleonic era' in *Changing World,* by Philip Sauvain, Stanley Thornes, 1992

The Napoleonic Wars, by Graham Mitchell, Batsford Educational, 1989

MORE ADVANCED BOOKS

1815: The Armies at Waterloo, by Ugo Pericoli, Sphere Books, 1973

'The Battle of Waterloo' in *Epic Land Battles,* by Richard Holmes, Octopus, 1976

'The Battle of Waterloo' in *The Decisive Battles of the Western World,* by J.F.C.Fuller, Paladin, 1970

The French Revolution and Napoleon, by Joe H. Kirchberger, Facts on File, 1989

The Life and times of Napoleon, by Mario Rivoire, Hamlyn, 1968

Wellington: The Years of the Sword, by Elizabeth Longford, Weidenfeld and Nicolson, 1969

Films

You may also wish to see on television or on video the movie *Waterloo* starring Rod Steiger, Christopher Plummer, Orson Welles, Virginia McKenna, Jack Hawkins, Dan O'Herlihy and Rupert Davies.

Index